The Secret Life of
Pancho Villa

Poems and Memories of Other Beloved Pets
DONALD DALE JACKSON
Illustrations by Koren Harpaz

Order this book online at www.trafford.com
or email orders@trafford.com

Most Trafford titles are also available at major online book retailers.

© Copyright 2011 Joyce Darlene (Hall) Jackson

All rights reserved. No part of this publication may be reproduced, stored in a retrieval system, or transmitted, in any form or by any means, electronic, mechanical, photocopying, recording, or otherwise, without the written prior permission of the author.

Printed in the United States of America.

ISBN: 978-1-4269-6898-3

Library of Congress Control Number: 2011909112

Trafford rev. 07/27/11

www.trafford.com

North America & international
toll-free: 1 888 232 4444 (USA & Canada)
phone: 250 383 6864 ♦ fax: 812 355 4082

Foreword

I am publishing this book for three reasons: (1) to share the joy that our family pets past and present have brought to us, (2) to memorialize those pets, and (3) to have a permanent record of the witty, loving, and sensitive words of my late husband, Donald Dale Jackson.

This story really began when Don and I were children. We each had a beloved pet. Don's family had a little Scotty named Terry who used to travel in his mother's pocket while she shopped. I heard so much about Terry, but he died before I met my husband's family. In my family it was my beloved Bootsie, a cat that shared my growing up years. She let me dress her doll clothes and push her around in my doll carriage. She, too, died before Don and I met, but we regaled each other with stories of the antics of our childhood pets.

Don and I were married on a weekend pass while he was in the Army and were immediately sent to an army base in Dundalk, Maryland. We lived in a little row apartment in this Baltimore suburb. While we were visiting with Don's grandmother (affectionately nicknamed "POG" for Poor Old Grandma by Don) in Virginia, we ventured into a pet store and acquired our first dog, a little white beagle who we soon came to love and called "Dinky." Sadly, Dinky's life ended prematurely when he ran into the street one day while we were moving. Don wrote a poem about how his death affected us, perhaps his first writing about a family pet.

After Don got out of the Army, we took a belated honeymoon to Europe. We sailed over by freighter, bought a used motor scooter when we got there and traveled about 6,000 miles throughout the continent between September 1960 and January 1961, creating many wonderful memories that we would share with our children for years to come. Upon return we settled in San Francisco and Don went to work for UPI on a split shifts – two weeks days, followed by two weeks nights, followed by two weeks overnights. I worked in miscellaneous part time jobs, but I spent many nights alone and wanted a little friend to keep me company. Following up on a grocery store sign about free kittens, I persuaded my dog-loving husband that he might like a cat. We picked the liveliest little male kitten there, and the saga of Pancho Villa began.

He was like our first child. We took him everywhere We tried to teach to him to walk on a leash (no good), took him for boat rides in Golden Gate Park, and to visit Don's family (also dog people, but they indulged us). Then Don was recruited to Life Magazine in New York City. During the move, we had to be temporarily housed with our beloved Aunt Peggy and the aforementioned POG in New Jersey. Unfortunately, POG was terrified of cats. Not just terrified – phobic. Poor Pancho had to stay in a kennel for several weeks. Each day I took Aunt Peggy's car to the kennel, where I would take Pancho out for a ride and try to convince him that we still loved him.

Finally our little family was moved into the city. In 1965 we added our son Dale to the family, and we got on fine - that is, we were all fine. But if you were a visitor to our apartment or, God forbid, a veterinarian, Pancho could be quite intimidating. One day Don took Pancho for his shots and came home splattered with blood. Pancho's attitude toward medical care did not improve with age. He would allow us to give him pills, medications, or even clip his nails, but no one else.

In September 1965 Don received a Nieman Award, and Pancho traveled with us to Harvard, where we lived until May 1966. It was during this time that Don wrote, "The Secret Life of Pancho Villa," borne of his imagination and affection for our unique pet. To create the characters in the story, he rearranged the letters in "Pancho Villa."

When the year ended, we visited family in California, then returned to New Jersey and Don returned to Life Magazine. It was during our tenure there that Bucky Mulligan became a member of the family. Bucky was a half Cairn, half Irish terrier, and cute as a button. Our growing family grew bigger still when our daughter Amy was born.

Don became a staff writer at Life allowing him to work from home, so on April 1, 1969 we bought and moved into our first and only home in Connecticut. To make the family complete, we soon added a lovely collie puppy, whom we named Holly Golightly. She was sweet, lady-like, and the perfect pet for our growing family, but Pancho remained at the top of the pecking order, and both dogs (and the children!) recognized this.

Ultimately, Pancho talked us into allowing him to prowl outside. Up to this point, he had been strictly an indoor cat. He became an eager hunter and brought home his "kills" for us. He became a night dweller, caterwauling and difficult to coax inside in the evenings when we wanted to shut down the house for the night. Sadly, this led to his demise, as he contracted leukemia from his adventures. (This was before there was a vaccination to prevent the disease.) It was a horrible, painful loss, which was followed closely by Bucky's death.

Bucky had been having a disagreement with another, larger dog in the neighborhood about who was in charge. From their previous altercation, he was wearing a bucket on his head – a design of the veterinarian's, to keep him from biting at the stitches on his neck. I put Bucky out on his lead in our back yard. In an attempt to keep the peace and keep Bucky safe, I had called the neighbor and asked her to keep her dog inside while I took a short run. Holly and I set out on our run, but halfway down our street, she stopped abruptly and began running back toward the house. We came home to find Buck in a bloody pile, in shock and near death. I scooped him up and rushed him to the vet, but he did not live through surgery.

Amy was in second grade when Pancho died and she wanted another kitten, so we adopted a beautiful little calico. We tried to name her Dynamite, but as things sometimes happen, over time her name became Olivia Newton Binkworth. We called her Binky.

Years passed and the children grew. In high school, our son Dale moved into a prep school about 45 minutes from home. During this time, Holly became ill with all of those mysterious, cruel conditions that begin to afflict the aged. Eventually Don had to take her for euthanasia. The loss of Holly Golightly was, collectively, perhaps the most difficult for our family to bear. I know it was for me. Don's memories of her and her gifts to us are here for you to read.

In Amy's last year of high school, while Dale was in college in California, Dulcinea joined the family. The name came from the show "Man of La Mancha," although she was truly more of an Aldonza. We were sold on Dulcie because animal welfare said she had collie in her. I don't think so. Whenever anyone asked, Don said she was a Bulgarian Inglebritz…but he made that up. She was one of a kind. She became Don's dog, riding in the car with him on all his errands, getting treats at the bank regularly, and living mostly outside between her house in the garage and the lead to the woods. She loved it out there. Before Amy left to college, she and Dulcie used to run together. When Dulcie died, Don took it so hard that he said he never wanted another dog.

We had a brief four - cat period. My mom and her cat Spatsy moved in with us in 1989, and Amy and her two new kittens, Phineas and Sabina, moved back home for a short while in 1990. Binky lodged several complaints about this, but Dulcie seemed not to notice. After Amy moved out and our pets passed, Don said he wanted another male cat. That is when Dugan, a frisky red tabby entered our lives.

Don died more than five years ago, and I was glad to have Dugan around. I think he was glad for me too. He greeted me each morning and when I came home. He lived 17 years, making mischief every one. It nearly killed me to put him down last spring when he became terminally ill, but that was the only way I could stop his pain. I still weep when I think of it.

Last spring my daughter took me to see some kittens in foster care. And thus began the next chapter, with my new cats Smokey and Bandit. I love them dearly, talk to them often, and don't know how I would exist without them. This collection is an homage to them, and to all of the loving pets that have made our life complete.

Joyce Darlene (Hall) Jackson

The Secret life of Pancho Villa
By Donald Dale Jackson

I had always thought of our cat, Pancho Villa, as nothing much more than, well a cat. He was big as cats go, he was sometimes vicious, he hated veterinarians, he had a strange habit of baring his teeth and making an ecccch sound when I snapped my fingers and pointed at him, but still and all he was just a cat.

A lot I knew. He was not merely Pancho Villa. He was also Ochnap Alliv, Emir of Baghdad! He was the notorious Dr. Huge, nuclear scientist and double agent! He was Phil von Laca, the richest baron in Bavaria! He was Calvin Phoal, an English professor, and he was Cecil Grimes, a Dallas fireman. He was not an ordinary pussycat.

It took a long time to figure out where he got the time to live all these other lives. In the first place, as far as I could tell he spent about 23 hours a day asleep. Not only that but he had never, in his four and a half years, been out of the house.

My wife explained it to me. Villa had what we called his house. It was sort of a traveling cage. It had a wooden floor and sides with a wire top and a hinged door. It was made for a cat or small dog. Villa would go into it every day. He would usually just check it out for a while and leave. Sometimes he would get comfortable and doze for a while. I thought that was all he was doing. Was I supposed to know that in those simple gestures he was becoming another being? But it seems that he has the power to leave his body behind while he himself the real Villa, or Alliv, or whoever he might be at that moment goes padding off to new adventures and conquests. It is like leaving a dummy in your bed while you skip out of the house, except that in this case the dummy is real. He seems to be there but somehow he really isn't.

My wife found out about it because Villa made a clumsy mistake. She was dusting his house one day when she suddenly screamed. I came steaming in from the living room and found her pointing at something in Villa's house and looking at me. She was pointing at some figures and letters and then an equals sign and then more figures, a parenthesis, a couple of lines and more letters.

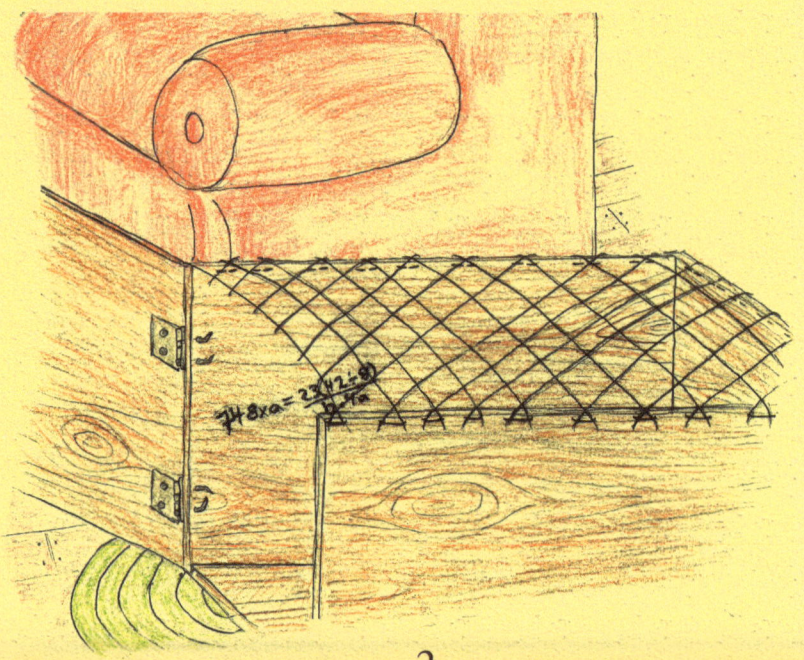

We were stunned. For a couple of weeks each of us suspected the other of sneaking into Villa's house and writing equations on his wall. I knew that I didn't do it. I barely made it through geometry in high school. I didn't think my wife did it either but what other explanation could there be? Certainly not . . . . no, certainly not.

A few days later he slipped up again. We find a tiny flower in a corner of his house. I've often wondered whether he wanted us to find out, and was planning these clues to give himself away. It seemed pretty clumsy to leave this little flower lying around his house.

And, I had never thought of him as clumsy, at least not clumsy in that way - he was never good at walking backward, it's true. Maybe he felt it was about time that we knew what he was really up to. At any rate this second clue turned out to be crucial.

The flower was a tiny gardenia about the size of a thumbtack. We had never seen anything like it. We knew instantly that it didn't belong to either of us. The only one who could have put that flower there was Villa.

For the next few days we poked around his house looking for more clues. One of us tried to stay awake all the time. I kept a small flashlight in bed with me so that if I heard anything peculiar I could shoot a beam at his house, which was right by the foot of the bed. We were nervous and worried, and there wasn't much laughter in the house. We looked at him differently now. We would be sitting in the living room and Villa would amble around the corner the same way he always did and we'd jump out of our chairs. Then he would look at us without curiosity, the way he always did, and leap to the top of the stereo, where he would stare out the window at the birds and other cats just the way he always did.

Our nervousness affected our son, who was only a year old. The baby was just learning to walk. Villa would come into the room, my wife and I would be surprised, and the baby would fall down. He'd noticed the tension. He'd try to run quickly, and down he'd go.

Villa didn't seem to go into his house as much as he had before. We knew that we couldn't go on this way, with everybody tense and the baby falling down. We decided to have a showdown. My wife and I put the baby to bed and sat in the living room, waiting for Villa to appear. When he did, we decided, we would simply ask him, straight out, to explain himself.

After about an hour he appeared. As usual he glanced at us without much interest and jumped onto the stereo. I walked over and pulled the blinds down so he couldn't see out the window. He gave me a warning bite on the wrist. I turned away and sat down again. My wife was leaning forward in her chair. Both of us were looking at Villa, and he was looking at us, evenly, his ears were alert, his tail tucked gracefully along his right side. He looked from one to the other of us.

I knew I had to say something. "Villa," I began, trying to sound stern. My wife looked at me anxiously. I really didn't know what to say. "Villa, there is something we've been wanting to ask you." I cleared my throat and looked at my wife. She nodded. Villa continued to stare at me. "Well, we were wondering about the writing on the wall of your house. And about the flower we found there . . . ." He jumped down and walked out of the room. I thought I saw him stop in the hall and start to turn back, as if he were reconsidering a hasty decision. But I may be imagining that. He didn't come back. We checked his house later but there were no more clues.

We didn't know what to do. There really wasn't anyone we felt we could talk to about it. You can't go up to someone and tell him you found this tiny flower in your cat's cage and that you think he might have some kind of secret life. For a while everyone was suspicious of everyone else. Villa still acted lovable sometimes. He slept as much as ever. We began to live with the mystery. We stopped talking about it and stopped jumping when he came into the room. The baby stopped falling down. Then Villa for reasons I'll never understand took the initiative.

It was about four o'clock in the morning. I was asleep, dreaming that I was sliding down a long, icy slope on my pants, and that I had tipped over and the side of my head was rubbing on the ice. I woke up feeling damp on my cheek and ear, and realized that Villa was licking the side of my face and rubbing me with his nose. As soon as he saw I was awake he jumped over to my wife's side of the bed and began doing the same thing to her. She awoke and we both looked at Villa. He looked quite awake, for him, and stepped back a few feet from my wife. He looked at us, one after the other, for a long minute and then jumped off the bed. He stopped at the door and looked back again.

I got up and followed him. He went first into the bathroom, jumped into the tub and sniffed around the faucet. Then he jumped out and went into the hall. Rubbing my eyes, I trailed a few feet behind him. My wife got up and joined us, and we formed an eerie column, stalking the house single-file in the blackness, the cat in the lead. He went into the kitchen, walked over to his food bowl and looked at it for a few seconds but didn't eat anything. I felt certain that something was coming.

He walked up to the pantry door, which was ajar, and pushed it open with his nose. It was dark and cold so I turned the light on. Villa stopped and looked at me, blinking in irritation. I turned the light off. Then he made an incredible leap, higher by far than I'd ever seen him jump before, up to the top shelf of the pantry, which was about three feet over my head and about eight feet over his. My wife never used that shelf because she couldn't reach it. I used it once, to hide a present for her. Villa sat on the shelf looking dignified. He drew himself erect and looked down at us, significantly, for about a minute. We stared back. My wife turned and looked at me.

Then Villa jumped down as quickly as he had jumped up and scurried out of the pantry. This time, obviously, we weren't supposed to follow him. We stood there for a few seconds and then I turned the light on again. My wife looked irritated, but I left it on. Maybe it was a crazy impulse, maybe it was a logical deduction, maybe it was an accident for whatever reason I reached up to the shelf where Villa had been. I had to stretch to do it, and for a few moments I didn't find anything but dust. Then I felt something else. It seemed to be some kinds of paper. I was beginning to get excited. I got a chair and stood on it to see what I had.

On the shelf was a pile of small pieces of paper, neatly stacked. Some of them were held together with paper clips. The sheets were the size of very small notebook paper, about two inches by three.

I took them down. My wife looked at me suspiciously. We walked into the kitchen, then into the hall. There was no sign of Villa. It suddenly seemed very important to find him. I wanted him to be there when we looked at his papers. My wife looked in the bedroom and bathroom, I checked the living and dining rooms. We both looked in the baby's room. We couldn t find him.

We sat on the couch in the living room and began to look at the papers. They were filled with very small writing, so small that it was almost impossible to read. It seemed to be some kind of diary. There were entries for each date. It went back two years.

We got a magnifying glass and read it all the way through, sitting there on the couch at four in the morning. I would read a page and then pass it to my wife. It turned out there there were about 60 sheets of thin, tissue-like paper. When we had finished Villa appeared from underneath the couch. He looked, well, I guess you could say proud.

The diary told the story. On Mondays, it seems, he was Phil von Laca, millionaire playcat, known in Acapulco, and Nice and St. Moritz and New York. The Monday entries were colorful, romantic, and confident. Sometimes the writing was a little wobbly as if is it possible? he had a bit too much champagne.

Baron Phil von Laca, Millionaire Playcat

Tuesdays he was a tweedy Calvin Phoal, the English professor the girls all adored, a bachelor, steady, reliable, and intelligent.

Calvin Phoal, English Professor

Wednesdays he was Dr. Huge, whose life was a web of espionage, betrayal, midnight meetings and sudden journeys, a cat that no one could trust, but everyone, it seemed, needed.

Dr. Huge, Scientist

Thursdays he was Ochnap Alliv, the emir. His subjects swooned at his feet. His robes were silk. He received his weight in jewels (12 pounds) once a month.

Achnap Alliv, the Emir

Fridays and this is the one that was hardest for me to believe he was Cecil Grimes, a fireman, of all things, in Dallas. This was especially surprising because the one time that I saw Villa around - fire - some grease on the stove flared up - he lowered his ears, stuck his tail in the air and bolted off in a convincing show of panic.

Cecil Grimes, Fireman

The diary did not go into detail on how he managed the transportation, or how he was able to convince us that he was around all the time when he was really in Baghdad or Dallas or some other place. On weekends, I guess, he was content to be Pancho Villa, house cat. And now that I think about it I feel a little grateful. He certainly didn't have to stay home weekends. And if I had the kind of choices he does, I'm not at all sure I would.

Villa is walking toward me as I write this. He looks just like himself, I mean just like he always has looked. Now he's looking at me angrily. I promised him, you see, that I would keep his secret. But I don't know what he's worried about anyway. I have the impression that he can be whoever or whatever he wants to be. I wasn't going to mention this, but this morning I found the diagram of a football play on the wall of his house.

Holly Golightly, Bucky and young Dale Jackson.

Picture of BuckMulligan, our terrier

*Olivia Newton Binkworth
– Photo by DaleJackson*

Dulcinea, our last dog

Golightly
Written April 28, 1983
By Donald Dale Jackson

We named her Holly Golightly, a bit preciously it seems to me now, after the character in Truman Capote's Breakfast at Tiffanys. I don't remember much about Capote's Golightly, but ours was shy and gentle and dignified and ladylike to a fault. She was a splendid collie of modest and retiring disposition and protective instincts. Today I took her to the vet to be euphemistically "put to sleep."

The last couple of weeks, her last couple of weeks, were hideous. Her senses failed one by one with what seemed to me to be lightning speed. One day she couldn't see. Another day she couldn't hear. Then she couldn't walk or finally, even get up. At the end she didn't appear to sense our presence when one of us was nearby, trying in the feeblest and most helpless way to be some comfort to her.

The vet had advised us a couple of weeks ago that we "might want to consider the alternative" of have her *overanesthesized* and thus relieved of her pain. And ours. We didn't want to consider that alternative. With all the medication she was taking it seemed at least possible that something would help, if only slightly, that she might at least be a little more comfortable or a little more lively than she was otherwise and that she might therefore enjoy a few more days of precious life. I don't relish the role of deciding if and when it is "merciful" to end what appears to be an animal's suffering. Who knows how much pain there was, or what she wanted, or whether she could bear any more of it? I don't. I didn't. I did understand clearly how much of the suffering was actually ours. We had to listen to her gasps and pitiful dry-mouthed yips and whines, night and day for the final few days. It was difficult to work or to sleep or to think about anything else but the noise and and the misery it seemed to mean. I know that the decision to end the agony was for our sake as much if not more than hers. I can live with that, but it isn't easy.

Another thing the vet said was that he didn't think we would want to remember her the way she was in the last weeks. As feeble, appallingly thin, as blindly lurching around the family room bumping into walls and furniture, as pathetically crumbling to her knees and then rolling over on her side when she couldn't stand. Her eyes began to look filmy all the time, and one day there was a streak of fluid running down from her eye that looked exactly like a tear.

But I'm not worried about the way we'll remember her. We moved into this house 14 years ago when our children were four and one and we got Holly a couple of months later. She was with us the entire time we lived here, she was part of the house, and her lifetime spanned most of the years both kids have been alive and about a third of ours. There's a lot to remember in those years besides the last few weeks.

The way she stood at the top of the driveway in front of house, regal as a borzoi, ears at attention and tail swaying rhythmically, in charge, on her turf, greeting friends and repelling strangers with a husky bark that became more and more shrill as she aged. It was a long walk from the road up the driveway to the house and she didn't always choose to make it. In the early years, of course, she'd run up, but as time passed she became more selective about the way she invested her energy, and she often was content to let me get the mail and to meet me halfway on the way back. When we'd reach the lawn she like to dart and pivot around in little circles, leaping up and down erratically liked a puppy or some joyous child. When she did that you were supposed to run either at her or away from her and she'd tear off at an angle and then stop, stiffening her forelegs and planting her paws on the turf in preparation for another sprint. She would not always play this game, just when she felt so moved, and sometimes it came as a surprise because she would be loafing and dragging along and then suddenly burst into her crazed little dance. The last one was perhaps two or three months ago.

She could marshall all her natural dignity in defiance of anyone who attempted to insert something, directly, into her mouth. She wasn't, her manner seemed to say, that kind of a dog. I never knew a dog that would not take a bone or a piece of meat from somebody's hand, or any other place he could get it, but Holly absolutely refused, temptation be damned. If she was going to take anything in her mouth she would put it there herself, and that was that. When we had steak she sat by the table waiting and salivating like your average spaniel or terrier and when we got up to go to the porch with a bone in hand she'd leap for the door and run happily outside and then turn and look at us. But the prescribed move then was not to place the bone in her mouth—she would turn away, appalled—but to put it on the steps or the lawn. She would then pick it up, in her own way and in her own time. She would glance back gratefully and then trot off to partake in the mysterious ritual of dog and bone.

I remember taking her on a trip one time to a rustic resort in Massachusetts—she always vacationed with us and loved camping and hiking more than anything. She'd actually walk ahead when we hiked until she got so far in advance of the rest of us that she'd get worried and come back wondering where we were. She would never walk behind, and she'd always stay on the trail. In the last few years she got canny in her hiking style like she did on driveway patrol. She'd take off just like she always did but after a few hundred yards she'd drop off, without drawing attention to herself, and retrace her steps back to the starting point. She seemed to make an assessment of what was involved and would estimate her energy and make a decision, yes or no. When my wife and I took her with us on a ramble through a wildlife preserve a few months ago we had to keep her between us because she kept trying to turn and retreat. She showed what she thought of this by sitting down and refusing to budge. If we encouraged her and made rash promises she would get up for a few minutes and lope along in the old familiar way, but then she'd have second thoughts and turn around again.

On the trip to Massachusetts she showed us for the first and only time that she had no more interest in swimming than in taking things in her mouth. There was a pool and all of us were splashing round in it while Holly patrolled the border, alert as always for intruders. The temptation to pull her in was irresistible, and we nudged her into the water. She immediately sank to the bottom with an expression of terror and betrayal on her face, and when we got her back to the surface she gave us a withering look and made straight for the side. All of her fur was of course plastered to her body and she looked surprisingly thin and insubstantial. She shook herself off, stayed a few yards away from us for the rest of the afternoon and remained clear of pools or any other water for the rest of her life. A few years later we were walking along a beach in Nova Scotia and watching a German shepherd gambol merrily in the surf. Holly showed no interest in this. When the kids started running in and out of the water, only a few feet at a time, Holly ran up the edge of the waves and barked, refusing to go any farther and declaring her disapproval.

She was a splendid camper, the best and least demanding and most faithful and willing. Except possibly for the time we were in a tent in the Adirondacks and a bear moseyed by after all of us had bedded down in our sleeping bags. The bear was about 30 feet from the tent door, walking along the edge of a lake in search of our food, which was stashed in our canoe about 50 feet out for just that reason. I saw the bear sniff and lurch into the water toward our canoe. Until then no one else had seen it, but now I felt I had to yell to protect our food and so I did. The bear turned and looked at me in surprise and splashed out of the water. Everybody in the tent was now of course up and chattering nervously about the bear, but Holly was invisible. She had undoubtedly sniffed the bear before I saw it but she'd stayed quiet about it, and now she was making herself as small as possible in a pile of clothes. Not a bark, nothing. Holly wasn't messing with any bear, and she didn't even want to discuss it.

I never saw Holly bite anyone. Maybe it was the old aversion to taking anything at all in her mouth, but she was the least violent dog I have ever known. For Holly a curl of the lip and slightest exhibition of teeth was a display of rage. I never saw her curl her lip at a person and only once or twice at another dog, and I vaguely remember only one scuffle of any kind with another dog, that with a collie who showed up on her turf. The lip curl was mainly reserved for the cat, on the occasions when the cat made a mistake of coming too close to Holly's food bowl or irritated her by walking over her when she was lying down. That was it. Holly came in peace, professed nonviolence all her life, and left in peace—quietly, without any undue fuss and with dignity.

When she began to fail she seemed primarily perplexed that she couldn't do what she had always done. Each time she fell she tried to get up without help and seemed embarrassed about needing help, as she had seemed so embarrassed about so many things. Making her morning toilet, for example. It annoyed her if anyone was watching, and to avoid this she would vary her route from the house to the surrounding woods, going different places and remaining on the move while she made her deposit as if afraid to be caught in the act. In the final weeks we sometimes took her outside and had to stand by and be ready to catch her if she toppled, but still she tried to act as if she were alone and enjoying the privacy she deserved.

The hardest parts of listening to her pant and cry and yip in distress and were being abjectly helpless to do anything to relieve her. In the end not even being there, stroking her and talking to her was much comfort. She was, finally utterly and completely dependent, and her constant plaints seemed to be a protest against this ultimate embarrassment.

We made the final decision last night and took her to the vet this morning. Forty dollars to be cremated, no burial, no witnesses at the execution. She lay on the back seat of the car as limp as a blanket and motionless, her eyes blank and her bones prominent through the sable fur. I lifted her out of the car and handed her to attendant who took her away, and I didn't think to give her a final touch or pat or even to say something in farewell, in gratitude and love. This is my farewell, Holly, thanks and goodbye.

Our beloved Holly Golightly
Photo by Dale Jackson

Young Dugan

Adult Dugan

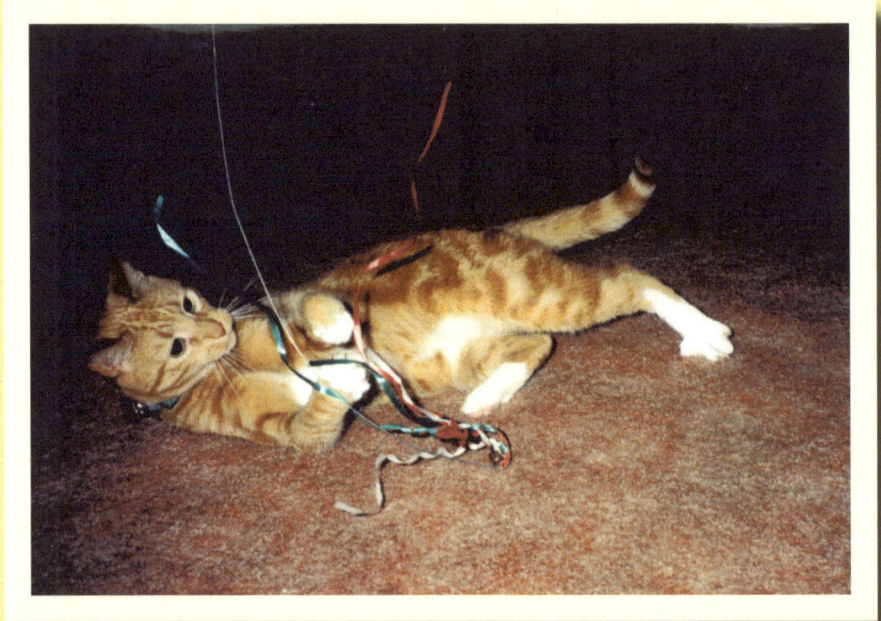

Finally, a picture of Dugan inspiring the poems by Don, who is pictured at his manual typewriter.

Cannonball Cat
(The Feline Projectile)

Who's that arching through the air
With such aplomb, such savoir faire?
Who rockets toward the stratosphere
And comes down 20 miles from here?
Who stays so cool and flusters not
When from a cannon he is shot?
Who climbs into the biggest gun
And grins because he thinks it's fun?
Who dares the muzzle's mighty roar,
Gets up, and sashays back for more?
Who spits at death and growls defiance
At mankind's murderous appliance?
Whose valiance do we celebrate,
Whose cheerful boldness venerate--
Let the name issue forth with a loud rat-tat-tat:
The Feline Projectile, CANNMONBALL CAT.

The Ballad of Piff Nifflemuff

Piff Nifflemuff's the shortest cat
Who works at Pam's Salon of Beauty.
For Piff, the only problem is
She has to stretch to do her duty.

For Pam and all the other girls
Who clip and trim and wash and chat
The job's a breeze, but not for Piff--
She's just a shade too short and fat,

When Mrs. Proudfur needs a perm,
Alas, it's not to Piff she goes.
The poor dear, even at full height,
Can't reach that stately lady's nose.

It was plain to Pam and all the rest
That Piff, despite unquestioned skill
At feline beauty care, was through--
Her chances of success were nil.

What happened next, I'd have to say,
Confirms again love's perfect power
To cut right through our petty plaints
And save us in the final hour.

Piff's boyfriend, Rodney, stout like her,
Volunteered to fill the breach.
Nowadays, Piff stands on Rodney's back
And every hair's in easy reach.

Piff Nifflemuff's Plight

The Blue Diamond Cat

Pull up a chair and I'll tell you the tale of the old Blue Diamond cat.
I think it's a story you'll take to your heart but you'll be the judge.
It started some 35 years ago at a place on the Jersey shore,
An old wooden dance hall perched on a pier that braved the ocean's roar.

The place was called the Blue Diamond, and at first it was crowded and gay--
The patrons stood in line for hours to revel the night away.
There were rotating bands and a stage with blue lights and singer named Rita McTigh
With a voice so tender and velvety soft that it almost made you cry.

When Rita was on, a curious scene took place on those long-ago nights:
A calico cat in a shiny blue ribbon sat near the edge of the lights,
And when her voice hit a certain note, the cat raised its head and cried,
And Rita would look at her songmate with conspiratorial pride.

The cat would sing only with Rita, the others it seemed not to see,
And when Rita bowed off the cat quickly bolted and hid in the backstage debris,
It was strange that the calico never got hungry, for nobody saw it eat,
And nobody knew its name or its sex, to make the puzzle complete.

As the years slid by the Blue Diamond changed, and crowds didn't come any more,
The building itself seemed to creak and sag, and water sloshed up through the floor.
Rita still sang for the few who showed up, and the cat still sang along,
But it wasn't the same, they'd stayed too long, and the beauty was gone from their song.

One night Rita couldn't go on, and nobody even asked why.
They found her dead in her dressing room, with a bottle of pills nearby.
Late that night the folks at the bar heard the tread of feline feet--
They saw the cat pause near the stage, then beat a fast retreat.

It was just a few weeks later that the Diamond closed for good,
The blue lights blinked their last, all that was left was rotting wood.
But still, each night from amid the dust came a strange cry like moan:
Dressed in its tattered blue ribbon, the cat sang its song alone.

Rita McTigh and the Calico Cat

Deputy Whiteshoes, Cat on Call

Deputy Whiteshoes, cat on call,
Waits alertly in the hall.
Costumed in his snappy cap
And badge, he fights the urge to nap
(Though sometimes, it is true, he loses
and yields to five-minute snoozes).
But normally for duty's sake,
He nags himself to stay awake.
Whiteshoes comes at ten at night
And stays until the sky grows light;
He's there to save the kids abed
From ghosts and every nighttime dread.
It's not as easy as it sounds;
Each hour Whiteshoes makes his rounds,
With canted head and nose aquiver
Listening for the slightest shiver.
But when dawn comes, and children rise,
Whiteshoes gets to close his eyes.
He washes, take off badge and hat,
And sleeps like a contented cat.

Deputy Whiteshoes, cat on call

Duane, the Desert Cat

Duane, the desert cat, quietly prowls
The sagebrush at night, neath the gaze of the owls.
He sidles through sand dunes and dusty dry sinks
And never lets anyone know what he thinks.
He goes his own way with a twitch of his ears,
Does his business obscurely, and then disappears.
Friendless he is, but he seems not to mind,
For Duane was never the sociable kind.
His dealings with others are sober and brief:
He eats them for breakfast, or runs like a thief,
But on some nights Duane lets his loneliness show,
In a way that suggests he wants someone to know--
Especially on nights when the mice meet for fun,
When they laugh and tell stories and dance until one,
If you look closely then maybe ten yards away,
Where the moon cuts the sand with a silvery ray,
You'll see cat eyes aglow under pointy cat ears,
And sometimes you'll see just a trace of cat tears.

Duane, the Desert Cat

Gladwin, the Playcat

Gladwin, the playcat, alone at the bar,
Looks somewhat disheveled and well below par.

His vest is unbuttoned, his boutonniere droops,
His whiskers are twisted in unseemly loops.

Gladwin grows surly when friends stop to chat;
They go away muttering, ill-tempered cat!

The truth is that parties and balls in high style
Can get to be wearisome after a while;

The life of a playcat may seem quite sublime,
But in fact it's a pain a good part of the time.

Sure, it's Gladwin, you're precious, and Gladwin, how droll,
But that won't do much for a cat's tortured soul;

Poor Gladwin is torn, he's betwist and between--
He wants to be loved and he wants to be seen.

His solution's a tradeoff, as so many are:
He parties til midnight, then broods at the bar.

Gladwin, the Playcat

The Night Deposit Cat

Have you seen those eyes that shine so bright
In the all-night drawer at the bank?
Have you heard soft steps as you turn away
And a faint but telltale clank?
The darkened bank is an eerie place
With the money all stashed away,
But that's when the Night Deposit Cat
Appears, and wants to play.
No one knows where he spends his days
Or how he gets in and out,
But every night, when the bank's locked tight,
He's inside, roaming about
Sometimes he growls to alarm the folks
Who use the all-night box,
Or he'll poke a paw through the slot and wave,
And scare them out of their socks.
Each morning, when the staff comes in,
They search the bank completely,
But the Night Deposit Cat's too smart--
He comes and goes discreetly.
Just once a note was found inside--
At least, so I've been told.
It said, Please turn the furnace up,
At night this bank's too cold.

The Night Deposit Cat

Smokey and Bandit, current companions

www.ingramcontent.com/pod-product-compliance
Lightning Source LLC
Chambersburg PA
CBHW040100160426
43193CB00002B/35